THIS
BOOK
WILL (HELP)
MAKE YOU
HAPPY

First published in Great Britain in 2021 by Wren & Rook
Text © Suzy Reading, 2021
Illustrations © Alex Paterson, 2021
Design copyright © Hodder & Stoughton Limited, 2021
All rights reserved.

ISBN: 978 1 5263 6315 2
E-book ISBN: 978 1 5263 6316 9
10 9 8 7 6 5 4 3 2 1

Wren & Rook
An imprint of Hachette Children's Group
Part of Hodder & Stoughton
Carmelite House
50 Victoria Embankment
London EC4Y 0DZ
An Hachette UK Company
www.hachette.co.uk
www.hachettechildrens.co.uk

Publishing Director: Debbie Foy
Managing Editor: Liza Miller
Art Director: Laura Hambleton
Senior Designer: Sophie Gordon
Designer: Clare Mills

Printed in England

Additional images supplied by Shutterstock

THIS BOOK WILL (HELP) MAKE YOU HAPPY

SUZY READING

ILLUSTRATED BY **ALEX PATERSON**

wren
&rook

CONTENTS

IT'S OKAY NOT TO BE OKAY

Everyone wants to be happy. There are lots of people who care about your happiness – your family, friends and teachers all want you to be happy. But sometimes we can feel pressure to be happy, and worry when we're not. But it's okay!

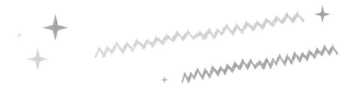

We all experience lots of different feelings. If you feel a little blue, or a bit confused, that's fine. Feelings aren't permanent. In time, things will change and you'll soon have a smile on your face again. When we fall out with a friend, it's normal to feel sad or upset about it. When we're faced with a difficult subject at school, it's normal to feel stressed or frustrated. Let's be super clear – we're not aiming to be happy all the time. It's just not possible, and actually it wouldn't be good for us.

All our emotions are okay! It's what we do with them that counts.

While it's totally normal and healthy to feel all our emotions, it's also okay to want to feel better. The tips and tools in this book will help you deal with difficult situations, and when you want to change how you feel, they will help you to feel happy, confident and calm.

10 CLUES **TO FIGURE OUT FEELINGS**

1. Life would be boring without feelings, and (even worse), we would not be healthy! Emotions are part of our **ESSENTIAL SURVIVAL TOOLKIT**, keeping us safe and helping us live together.

2. Feelings are **SIGNALS** from our bodies, alerting us to check in and take action to keep ourselves safe and healthy. Fear pops up, telling us there could be danger. We feel angry when we, or things we value, are threatened. This helps us to defend ourselves. We feel sad when we lose something special, reminding us to take time out to feel better. Guilt taps us on the shoulder, reminding us to check in with what's right and what's wrong. Loneliness tells us that we need to be with people. When you think about your feelings as messengers, you can see why **EVERY** emotion has its place and purpose.

3. You have emotions. They are not **WHO** you are. Feelings pass, just like the weather changes. They come and go, and it's our job to take a look at what they're saying to us and then choose how we respond to them.

4. Feelings are not facts. Our emotions don't always reflect the truth of the situation. Sometimes that mixed-up feeling in our stomach is hunger, not something to worry about. We have to figure out what feelings mean. Excitement, anticipation and nerves can all feel pretty similar!

5. Feelings aren't good or bad. Some emotions feel lovely, some are just okay, and others can be hard to deal with. But because every emotion has a **MESSAGE** for us, we need them all. Labelling them as positive or negative doesn't really help us, and only aiming for the pleasant ones doesn't work well for us either.

6. So, if we're not aiming for constant happiness, what are we aiming for? Recognising our feelings is a good start. Having a wide range of words to describe how we feel helps us identify our emotions and express ourselves.

7. Make a list of all the emotions you can think of. Here's some **INSPIRATION** for you: happy, joyful, pleased, content, amused, excited, energetic, restless, surprised, disgusted, bored, angry, frustrated, irritated, annoyed, grouchy, loving, tender, kind, embarrassed, guilty, scared, anxious, nervous, unsure, jittery, sad, lonely, heartbroken, hopeful, peaceful, calm, reflective.

8. To help you notice different feelings, ask yourself what emotions characters might be feeling when you're reading a book or watching TV. There can be many all at once.

9. Try this exercise with your family. Describe your feelings and then ask others to describe how they are feeling. You will notice that it isn't always easy, even for grown ups! When someone mentions a feeling that you don't understand, look it up in the dictionary and add it to your list.

10. When you're feeling sad or upset, **CHECK IN** with your list to help you name your emotions. Just identifying your emotions can help you feel more in control of them.

TOP FIVE WAYS TO GET YOUR THINKING STRAIGHT

1. You are not your thoughts. We all have a stack of thoughts that pulse through our brains. Some are useful, while others are unkind or scary – and it's totally normal to have them all. You can have a nasty thought and it doesn't make you a nasty person.

2. Don't believe everything you think! Thoughts are **NOT FACTS** and they don't predict the future.

3. There's no point trying to clear your mind. Even though those pesky thoughts are normal, we need ways to manage them, because they can make us unhappy. Have you ever tried to get rid of a particular thought? It's a tricky business! Your brain is a **THINKING MACHINE** – it's designed to think, just as your eyes are designed to see. Your eyes will see lovely things and they will see some not-so-nice things, but you don't get cross with your eyes for seeing. So, don't get cross with your brain for thinking, it's just doing its job!

Have you noticed that trying to get rid of a thought sometimes makes it even bigger and louder? It can start to feel like a cheeky monkey getting cheekier the more we try to push it away. Rather than trying to empty your mind or get rid of a thought, give your mind something helpful to think about instead.

4. If unpleasant thoughts creep in, notice them and say **'HEY, I SEE YOU!'** Have a laugh – you might be amazed at the silly things your brain comes up with – then give your mind something else to focus on. Think of statements such as, 'I am doing my best', 'it's just a thought', 'I choose to be kind' or 'I am calm' (make up your own!). This might be hard at first, but it will get easier with practice.

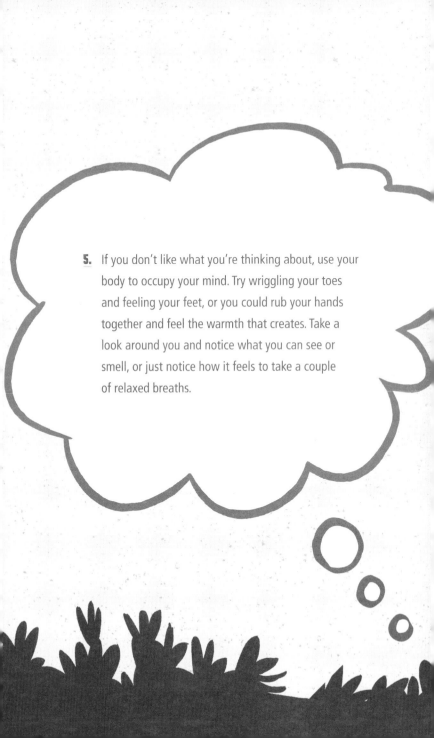

5. If you don't like what you're thinking about, use your body to occupy your mind. Try wriggling your toes and feeling your feet, or you could rub your hands together and feel the warmth that creates. Take a look around you and notice what you can see or smell, or just notice how it feels to take a couple of relaxed breaths.

YOU DON'T HAVE ^TO ^DO
IT ON YOUR OWN

While there are lots of different ways you can help yourself feel better, it's also really important to know that you don't have to do it on your own.

Everyone needs the **LOVE** and **SUPPORT** of others around them. It's always good to ask for help, so reach out and talk to someone. When we're brave and let others know how we're feeling, we encourage them to do the same, so we can be a safe place for them, too. Being there for each other is what draws us together as human beings.

When we're in the middle of a problem it's sometimes hard to see solutions. We need someone outside of the problem to help us think of things to try. Having someone just to **LISTEN** can be all you need to find your own solutions, too. It's okay to let people know what you need. This could be support and

understanding, company, a distraction, a kind ear, a hug, someone to brainstorm solutions with, or to just be in it together. Don't **BOTTLE IT UP**! A problem shared really is a problem halved.

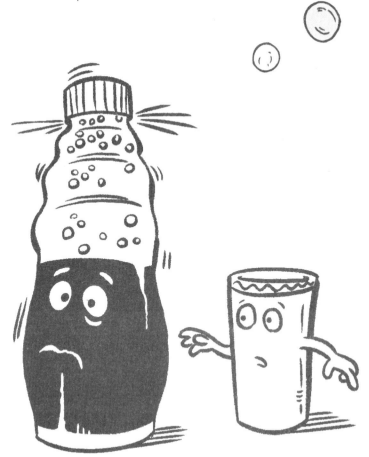

So, who can you go to when you need help working out a tricky emotion or problem? Think of all the people in your life who are there for you. These might be parents or carers, siblings, grandparents, aunts, uncles and cousins, friends, teachers and club leaders. Or if you prefer, you can call or email one of the groups below:

Kidscape.org.uk

Childline.org.uk

Kidshelpline.com.au

Kidsline.org.nz

SHOT OF HAPPINESS!

If you're feeling down in the dumps, don't wait for tomorrow, your day can start again in an instant. It's time for some fun!

COUNTDOWN TO BOOSTING YOUR HAPPINESS

3. **Find your chicken wings.** Feeling tired? Got what I call the 'grizzle grumps'? Get out your chicken wings. Trust me, I know this sounds ridiculous, but find somewhere private to do it and you'll feel great afterwards. Place your fingertips on your shoulders, forming the chicken wings. As you breathe in, circle your elbows forwards and up, and as you breathe out, circle them backwards and down. Repeat six times for good measure. Make that wing action as big as you can, feeling it open your chest, releasing tension in your shoulders and making you feel super tall. Notice how good it feels to take a few deep breaths, too.

2. **Shake it off.** Stand tall with your feet shoulder-width apart and your arms floppy like cooked spaghetti. Swing your arms around to the right, twisting your torso to take it with them and looking over your right shoulder. Let your left heel lift so your hips can twist deeper to the right. Then swing it all to the left, allowing your right heel to lift. Repeat this floppy twist a few times on each side, imagining all the stuff that weighs you down sliding from your shoulders and flicking off from your fingertips. Shimmy, shake, twist about … just let it all go!

1. **Turn your world upside down.** Do a handstand and you'll see things from a fresh perspective. Head outside somewhere safe and see if you can kick your legs up. Can't get outside? You can use a wall in your home, just make sure you have enough space. There are no scores out of ten, it doesn't matter how it looks, just give it a go and see how it feels. Having trouble getting up? Don't worry! Try 'walking up the wall' instead. Sit with your back against the wall, legs outstretched. Notice the place where your feet reach this is where you will now place your hands, shoulder

width apart. Next, from all fours, take your feet back behind you and walk them up the wall until your spine and legs are parallel to the floor. This is hard work for your arms, so stay only as long as it feels good. Once you're down, whatever variation you tried, feel the blood pumping around your body and the smile now on your face!

BUILD YOUR MINDFULNESS MUSCLE

A clear, calm mind can help you to deal with the trickiest of emotions or peskiest problem – but what exactly is this 'mindfulness' thing?

Mindfulness is paying attention to the moment as it's happening – all the things around you and all the things inside you, which includes your thoughts, emotions, sensations and memories. It's more than just noticing, it's also letting things be as they are and not giving yourself a hard time for feeling as you do.

What's all the fuss about mindfulness? Well, it deserves to be centre stage for three good reasons:

1. When life gives you the squish, mindfulness allows you to step back, and choose what to do next without being so pushed around by your thoughts and feelings.

2. Mindfulness lies right at the heart of feeling **CALM** and **CONFIDENT**, because noticing how you feel right now in your mind and body is the first step to taking care of yourself.

3. Because mindfulness makes you notice everything, it helps you appreciate the people, places and things around you. Gratitude – feeling thankful – always makes you feel better. So, it really is worth your while building your mindfulness muscle. It's something we can all grow with practice.

HOW TO GET MINDFUL!

If you're thinking that mindfulness isn't for you, maybe you haven't found a mindful activity that floats your boat yet. Stick with it! Try these three ways:

1. The next time you're eating a treat you **LOVE**, don't do anything else at the same time. Feel how amazing this experience is with every one of your senses. The feel of it in your hand, the delicious smell, the touch of it against your lips, the zing of it hitting your taste buds, the texture of it as you roll it around your mouth, how it feels as you swallow … and how it fills you with joy!

2. When you next have a **HUG**, close your eyes and give it your full attention. Notice how cosy it feels to be held, to receive love and to give love. Can you feel your heartbeat, can you feel theirs? Breathe it in and let it fill you up with happiness.

3. Take a walk and get really curious about how your body feels to be moving. Feel your clothing against your skin, the warmth of the sun on your body or the **SENSATION** of the breeze. Notice how you are holding your shoulders, how long your spine is. Is there space between the top and bottom rows of your teeth? **FEEL** what it's like to swing your arms. Take some lovely long strides and **NOTICE** how that feels, the muscles that engage in your legs and the grounding of your foot with each stride. Just notice how it feels to be in your body.

JOURNAL YOURSELF HAPPY

Have you ever tried keeping a journal? Research has shown that writing down our thoughts can keep us happy and healthy – simple but amazing, hey?!

How many thoughts do you reckon a person has in one day? No one knows for sure, but it's loads – somewhere between 12,000 and 60,000! That's a whole lot of **NOISE**. How can we get a bit of peace and quiet in there? Put pen to paper. Evidence has shown that writing your thoughts down can **RELAX** your nervous system and help support your immune system. The act of writing boosts your happiness and health by helping you explore emotions and fine-tuning your communication skills. Focus your writing on uplifting themes such as hope and thankfulness and you've got yourself a powerful way to help you feel good.

33

Journalling, making notes or keeping a diary can be a powerful way to express yourself. Writing out what you are thinking and feeling can stop your thoughts and feelings from bouncing around in your head. It can help you make sense of them and give you a clearer picture of the way things really are. When you read back what you've written, it can help you to see what you actually need to think about, and what you can let go of, such as things that aren't real or haven't actually happened yet. It can also help you to focus on what you need to do to feel better.

Whenever you want to dump what's in your head, take out any old piece of paper and write down whatever comes to you. You could start simply with the question 'What's on my mind?' There's no right or wrong. It can be a healthy way to get rid of things you don't want to say out loud, things that might hurt other people. Get it out, scribble it down and then, really importantly, screw it up and toss it away. No need to keep it – reading back those words will only make you feel all that stuff again.

You can also use positive questions, such as 'What went well today?' Now, these are the entries we **DO** want to keep! Reading them later brings back the happy feelings! You can write about good things that have happened or things that you're looking forward to. Jot down your answers – they are there to be enjoyed again and again.

For the purpose of journalling positive things, you might want to keep an actual notebook that you love the look and feel of. Or, you could keep a folder or box of uplifting entries. Totally up to you. You can write when you feel happy, look for the **SILVER LININGS** (positive things in a not-so-good situation) when you feel sad, or just read back old entries and feel them lift you back up.

CHALLENGE ACCEPTED!

Want to start your day with a skip in your step? Then set yourself a goal.

Goals make us determined and focused. If there's something you'd like to achieve, you're more likely to achieve it if you set a goal. It will also help to build your self-esteem. Bonus!

COUNTDOWN TO SETTING GREAT GOALS

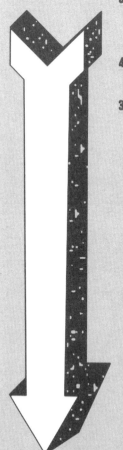

5. Make your goals about things that **YOU** want for **YOU**, not what someone else wants for you.

4. Choose goals that feel **IMPORTANT** to you.

3. Write them as a **POSITIVE** description of something you want to do more of, or achieve, rather than do less of, or avoid. So, a useful goal is 'I want to get along well with my sister,' rather than 'I want to fight less.' The word 'fight' primes your brain for what you don't want!

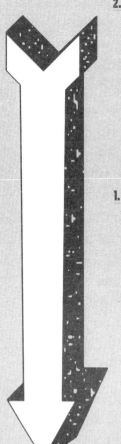

2. Make goals **REASONABLE** and **FLEXIBLE**.
A goal that's too easy doesn't really fire us up,
but equally, a really far-off goal can set us up for
failure. It should be a reach, but not a crazy
leap. We also have to keep it real in terms of
the time and energy we can devote to a goal.
Useful goals are ones that we can change in
response to what's happening in our lives.

1. If you have more than one goal at a time, make
sure they complement each other, not conflict.
That's a recipe for frustration! For example,
getting on well with your sister would work
well with getting better at a sport she
enjoys, too.

Grab your journal, it's time to set yourself a personal **CHALLENGE**. Is there a goal you'd like to work towards? It could be anything from learning to surf or memorising cool words in a new language, to drawing amazing manga cartoon eyes or playing your favourite song on the guitar.

Think about the kinds of skills or strengths that you'll need to draw on for your goal (see page 66 to get clear on yours). If your goal feels really big, break it down into little steps that you can tackle one by one. These steps will give you something to celebrate along the way. Think about possible obstacles and devise ways you can overcome them. Use your journal to track your progress and see how far you've come. Once you've achieved your goal, how will you reward all your effort? Happy planning!

**Let others know about your goal
so they can cheer you on! Is there
a friend you can ask to support you?**

MAKE GRATITUDE YOUR ATTITUDE

Turn that frown upside down by thinking about things to be thankful for. It'll make you feel great!

When you get really good at spotting opportunities to be **THANKFUL**, it changes how you see your day. It helps you to focus on the brighter side of life, rather than noticing only the things that niggle at you and get you down. A heartfelt thank you will make other people feel good, too – we all like to feel appreciated!

Even in grouchy moments, gratitude can help **LIGHTEN** your load. Feel annoyed about having to tidy your room? Gratitude helps you feel thankful for having a safe place to live. When your mind daydreams about all those things that you want on your birthday list, appreciation helps you enjoy what you already own.

This is one of the greatest keys to feeling content – enjoying your current blessings. When things go a bit **SKEW-WHIFF** gratitude can help you see the upside, even if it's just a chance to learn how things might go better next time. Finding good in a bad situation helps you to dust yourself off and move on.

You could use your journal to grow your gratitude skills. Write down or draw happy moments, or stick in messages from your friends.

Or you could create a gratitude jar – jot down things that make you thankful on small pieces of paper and pop them in your jar. Maybe it's the shady tree in your garden, the robin that comes to visit, a mug of hot chocolate, cuddles with your cat or a video call with Grandma. Whenever you need a lift, open up your jar and pull out one of your notes. You will always find something inside it to make you happy!

TAKE **FIVE**

One of the easiest ways to feel calm is to take a few relaxed breaths. But how does the way you breathe change the way you feel? It's all about the nervous system.

The nervous system includes your brain and carries **INFORMATION** about what's happening inside you and around you. The information helps you respond to what's happening and keeps you safe. When you feel upset or threatened, your body fires up the 'stress response', which helps you defend yourself or run away. In this stress-response mode, the heart beats faster, pumping blood away from your brain and organs to your arms and legs. It is really hard to think straight in this state!

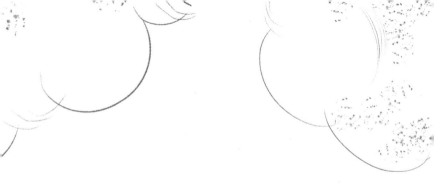

When you're feeling safe, relaxed and calm, the nervous system is in 'rest and digest' mode. This is when your heart rate is slow, your muscles are relaxed and your body can focus on digesting food and repairing itself.

The trouble is, sometimes when we're worried the body switches on the stress response and it doesn't help us in that moment. When you're about to turn over your quiz paper or shoot for that goal, the last thing you want your body to do is prepare to fight or run away … you need to stay put, think carefully and pay attention!

Breathe!

When you feel like you need soothing, try this super easy **TAKE FIVE** exercise. Hold out your hand and stretch it like a star. With the pointer finger of your other hand, trace the outline of your stretched hand, starting at the outside base of the thumb. As you breathe in through your nose, trace up to the tip of your thumb, pause a moment, and as you breathe out through pursed lips (like you're blowing out a candle), slowly trace down your thumb. Continue tracing up and down each finger. By the time you've finished, you've taken five slow, relaxed breaths. Do you feel a little calmer or do you want to take another five?

It's best to play with the Take Five exercise when you're already feeling happy and relaxed. Have a practice with it before you use it in stressful moments. Once it feels familiar you can use it whenever you start to feel irritated or worried. Notice how it can help you choose kinder words when your brother or sister is driving you nuts, or how it can help you take your time when you're focusing on schoolwork.

It can take some practice, but your breathing can be one of the most powerful ways to change how you feel. Taking a few relaxed breaths is like hitting a switch, turning on the calm mode where you can focus your mind and feel confident. It can even help you get to sleep. Breathe better to feel better! This is a superpower we all possess.

START YOUR MORNING RIGHT

The key to a happy start to the day is creating your own morning routine.

No one wants to feel hurried, nagged or grouched at in the morning. Routines give your day rhythm and regularity, which is relaxing for your mind. By reducing the number of choices you have to make, you save valuable energy and brain power for the rest of your day. Following a routine makes you feel well prepared for the day ahead, and can mean fewer arguments!

To prepare for your day you need to know what's happening in it. If you have regular activities in your week, you can create your own seven-day planner and keep it in your room. Write down the different clubs and things to do for each day and jot down what you need to take with you. If you want, you can write down the time you need to get up and the time you need to be ready by.

If every week is different, have a calendar set up for you to see, so you can check in and plan ahead.

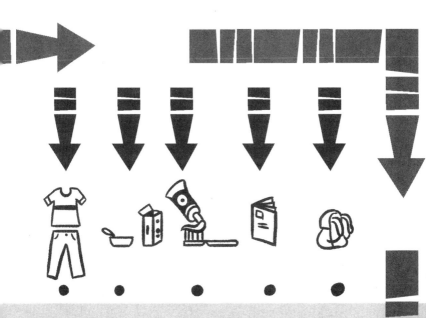

To start your morning right you have to begin the night before. Before you go to bed, **PREPARE** anything you need for the following day, such as your uniform, books, instruments or sports kit. Have your clothes laid out and bags packed so you can just focus on getting ready in the morning.

Write down what you have to get done in order, such as breakfast, teeth and getting dressed. You also could jot down what's nice to do if there's time, such as watching TV or reading. Focus first on what you have to get done (and remember it can take a bit of team work, especially if there's a queue for the bathroom!) Once you're ready, you can use any spare time for the nice things, and you'll feel **CALM** and in control when it's time to leave.

THE MAGIC (SLEEP) TRICK

Think about anything that's important to you in your day – such as playing football, paying attention in class or getting on with your mates. All of those things are improved by a good night's sleep!

'You snooze you lose.' Don't believe this for a moment! Some seriously amazing things happen when you're asleep. Sleep is essential for your mind and your body. It's when your body repairs, and restores, giving you the **REST** that you need to grow well. Your brain does lots of organising when you're asleep, too. It stores information and works through problems, which in turn sharpen your memory and help you to focus and learn the next day.

Just like we need a morning routine for a cheery start to the day, an evening **RITUAL** will make for a more peaceful bedtime and a better sleep. To design your ritual, jot down some ideas, and then start practising things that help you feel like your day is complete. You might get out your uniform and pack what you need for tomorrow. A quick tidy away can make your room feel more relaxing. Make sure you've got a fresh water bottle by your bed.

Next, prepare your mind and body for rest. Switch off screens an hour before bed and get ready for some soothing activities. It doesn't have to be the same ritual every night, but make sure there is something calming that paves the way for a peaceful bedtime.

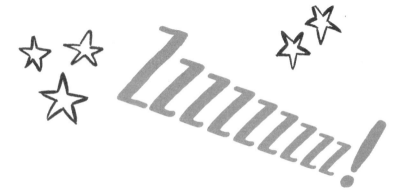

5 WAYS TO UNWIND

1. Get squeaky clean with a bath or shower. Remember to brush your teeth, too!

2. Pop on PJs that you love. This helps to prime your brain and body for sleep.

3. Try a little journalling to express your thoughts and feelings.

4. Some mindful colouring can soothe your mind if it's feeling busy.

5. Have a good stretch to ease away any tension in your body.

Hop into bed and let your body **FLOP** and **DROP**. If your mind is still feeling busy, read something relaxing, listen to music or just take some slow breaths, making sure they are nice and long. You can't make yourself sleep, so don't worry if it takes you a while to drop off or if you wake up. Remember, it's not only sleep that is helpful, relaxation is good, too! Just rest, sleep will come. And don't worry if you didn't get a great sleep. There's always tomorrow night.

DON'T GET HANGRY!

Hanger is real! You know that state when you get so hungry you feel cross? You feel hangry! Well, it's not just your body that needs fuel to function – your mind needs nourishment, too.

We need to be well fed and watered to think straight and feel calm. The next time you find yourself feeling snappy, jittery or just plain pooped, ask yourself: when was the last time I fed my brain? When was the last time I had a glass of water? Not drinking enough water has the same grinch-inducing effects as not eating.

What and when we eat is important. To make us feel really good, we need to eat fresh food at regular times. This should include fruits and vegetables in a rainbow of colours, because they each have different nutrients. Munching on a variety of food types helps to keep things interesting and makes sure that we get all the vitamins, minerals and everything else that we need to keep us healthy and happy.

Eat something filling and nutritious for breakfast, and you'll set yourself up for the day. Skip breakfast, and you'll run the risk of getting super-hungry. You might even find yourself reaching for the nearest sugary snack. It's harder to make healthy food choices when you're hungry because when your **ENERGY** is low, you are more likely to want salty, sugary and fatty foods.

Healthy options are **WHOLE FOODS**, such as fruit and veg, seeds, nuts, pulses and whole grains, rather than sugary foods that come out of a packet. If you have to look at the ingredients to find out what's in something, then it's usually not a great choice. Reach for fresh fruit or veg, cheese or a yoghurt rather than crisps or chocolate bars. Having some go-to snacks that you can rely on to feed your brain and body will make for a happier day.

Jot down the whole foods that help you feel good, and let your family know so they can keep the house well-stocked.

Give the person who does the food shop a heads up when supplies are running low, so you always have what you need to nourish yourself, mind and body.

Getting involved in shopping, food prep and cooking puts you more in control of how you look after yourself – and you'll make your family happy by helping at home, too!

GET **MOVING**
FOR YOUR **MIND**

Feeling down in the dumps? Have more worries on your mind than usual? Burn off that negative energy and get some movement in your day!

We all know exercise keeps our heart, lungs, bones and muscles healthy. But, did you know that it's also **REALLY** good for our mental health? We can blow away the blues with movement! Any movement can help make you smile, focus, and feel calm, as well as giving you energy. It doesn't matter what it looks like and you don't have to be 'good' at it!

Grab your journal and make a note of all the different ways you like to move your body – the more **FUN**, the better. Note down anything from geocaching, body boarding, karate, kitchen-disco sessions or roller-skating, to bouncing on a trampoline, yoga, riding a bike, swimming, kicking a ball, skipping, walking the dog or any of the exercises on page 63.

After you've finished moving in a way that makes you happy, write down how you **FEEL.** Next time you're feeling a bit down, go back to this list and pick an activity to do that you know will cheer you up. You can write about the other benefits you notice, too, such as the chance to connect with friends, time with your family, an opportunity to enjoy nature or a distraction from unhelpful thoughts. Physical activity can help you sleep better, too.

Your body and mind need daily movement, ideally 60 minutes of physical activity every day. It doesn't have to be competitive, it doesn't need to be hard and it doesn't need to be all in one go. Remember, these 60 minutes include all the stuff you are already doing anyway, such as walking to school, sports clubs and PE. The best way to fire up your motivation to move is to keep it fun and varied and keep the benefits fresh in your mind.

COUNTDOWN TO MOOD-BOOSTING HORMONES

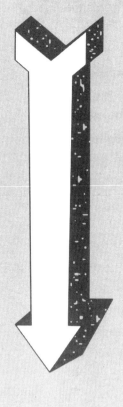

3. To get the happy hormones (such as serotonin and endorphins) flowing, research has shown that the most effective movement is walking, where you take long strides and give your arms a good swing. Skipping is great, too. Remember to keep your knees high. In fact, any movement where there's a sense of freedom with a tall, upright spine is great.

2. Stretchy, soothing exercise, such as certain types of swimming, dance, martial arts and yoga, is good for building your mindfulness muscles and letting go of worry and stress.

1. Do what you **ENJOY**!

WHAT'S YOUR SUPERPOWER?

Spelling, grammar, numbers, reading … it's really easy to get fixated on these things. They are important, but there are many different ways to shine! Although they might not be the topics of your school lessons, your other strengths and skills are just as valuable and useful in life!

Your **STRENGTHS** are the things you do well and enjoy doing. Just thinking and talking about them will give you energy. But how do we know what they are? You can think about the things you're good at and fill you with excitement, or you can ask your parents, carers or friends what they think you're good at. Write down all the different ways that you shine!

HERE ARE SOME IDEAS TO HELP YOU IDENTIFY YOUR STRENGTHS:

Bravery, speaking up for what's right, thankfulness, a sense of humour, playfulness, curiosity, enthusiasm, **positivity**, perseverance, **determination**, diligence, focus, being responsible, caring, kindness, honesty, a calming influence, loyalty, a great team member, a great leader, fairness, being careful, a love of learning, **adaptable**, flexible, forgiving, being organised, hopeful, faithful, communication skills, **understanding other people**, being creative, physical abilities, mental abilities (such as being good at strategy games) and humility.

Identifying your unique talents can help you feel good about yourself, and knowing your strengths can help you when things are tricky. Using your strengths feels fabulous! It helps to remember that we all have different superpowers and you don't have to be brilliant at everything. We all have things we do well and we all have things we need to work on, even the brainy bunch and the sports stars. Feeling down on yourself? Remember, you don't have to be perfect. You are enough! You have your very own superpowers that the world needs.

LOVE YOUR MISTAKES

Now you have identified your superpowers, let's look at building some new ones!

When you read through the list on page 66, did you notice any strengths that you'd like to own? Good news! You can develop every single one of them. You don't have to be naturally good at them to be able to master them. You just have to want to learn!

An essential part of learning any new skill is making mistakes. Everyone makes them, but how we feel about mistakes can make a huge difference. Mistakes are **NOT** the end of the world, and they don't mean that we can't do something or that we're not good enough. They just show us that something we tried didn't work … and information about what doesn't work actually helps us to find the solution that does.

Every mistake is an opportunity to learn something **NEW**. James Dyson, the inventor of the bagless vacuum cleaner, famously said: 'There were 5,126 failures. But I learnt from each one.' How's that for staying power?!

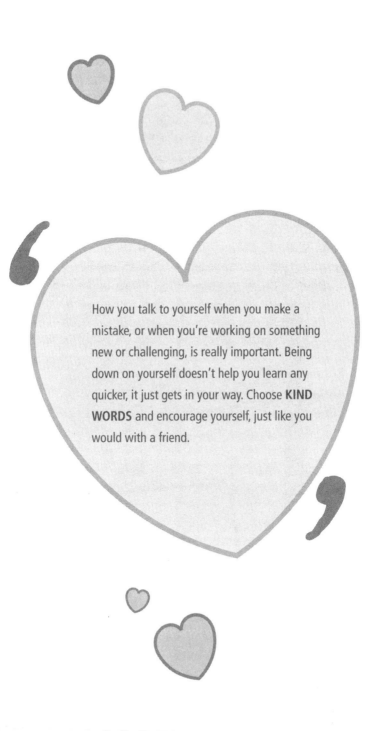

'How you talk to yourself when you make a mistake, or when you're working on something new or challenging, is really important. Being down on yourself doesn't help you learn any quicker, it just gets in your way. Choose **KIND WORDS** and encourage yourself, just like you would with a friend.'

COUNTDOWN TO BEING COOL WITH MISTAKES

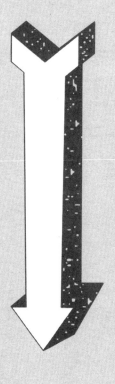

3. Switch up 'I can't' for 'I am learning to' or 'I haven't mastered it **YET.**'

2. Swap out 'I'm bad at this' and 'I'm rubbish at this' for 'I can get better at this with practice.'

1. When you make a mistake, get curious about it. Ask yourself: 'What did I learn?' and 'What could I do differently next time?' And remind yourself that it's okay to make mistakes. We all do! The key is to learn from them.

Remember, it's okay if you don't nail something first try. Keep going! We're aiming for progress not perfection and making progress can take time. Think how long it took you to earn your pen licence. Working on feeling brave, knowing your times tables or speaking in public is no different. Love all your mistakes – they help you to learn and grow.

IT'S WORRY O'CLOCK!

Although it's totally normal to worry now and again, there are ways you can make the worrying less, well, worrisome!

We all worry from time to time. But quite often, most of what we worry about doesn't end up happening anyway! Trying to stamp it out tends to make our worries bigger – and we can even get worried about worrying! A worry is just a thought, but it's pretty hard to get rid of a thought. So how **CAN** we work on our worries?

Rather than being poked and prodded by worries all day long, take control and set aside **WORRY TIME**. This is a specific time to sit with all your worries and the feelings they bring. Think about how long your Worry Time will be, where you might like to spend it and any strategies that help you deal with your worries. It might be as short as five or as long as twenty minutes, and a safe, quiet space, such as your bedroom, might feel good.

Finding a worry partner or writing things down can also really help. Enlist Mum, Dad or another adult you trust to take a look at your worries with you. Sometimes saying worries out loud is all it takes for us to see they're not real. Writing them down can be another way of getting things off your chest and can help you make more **SENSE** of your feelings.

As well as noticing worries, you could brainstorm solutions, or just think of things to try in situations that feel hard. A really important question to ask is: 'Can I do anything about this?' If it's beyond your control, no amount of worrying is going to make a difference, so it is a waste of your time and energy. If you can't do something about it, who can? **REACH OUT** to them for help and bring your focus back to what you can do something about. This will help you feel more powerful.

REACH OUT FOR HELP

When a worry pops up outside of your Worry Time, don't say to yourself 'Don't worry' (which we know doesn't work). Instead, say 'Not now, I have time for you later.' This is how we stop our concerns from spilling out and taking over our day. Quite often, the thing that was bothering you in the morning might not feel so big and scary later on, and sometimes, when you get to your Worry Time, you won't feel like worrying at all – and that's great! But if you do, that's okay, too. Take a look at what's bothering you, come up with a plan of attack, be kind to yourself and when the time is up, it's up! Move on and do something else.

RELEASE THE PRESSURE

Feeling the pressure with a test coming up? Anxious when you have to try something new? Well, we have ways of dealing with all of that!

Putting your hand up for school council, school plays, tournaments or teams to join … these experiences are all just part of life. Just like worry is normal, feeling a sense of pressure is totally normal, too. We all need some powerful tools to help us manage stress.

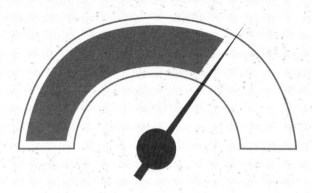

COUNTDOWN TO COMPOSURE

Below are a bunch of things to help you feel calm and composed. Different things will work at different times, so experiment, and if one thing doesn't work, try another!

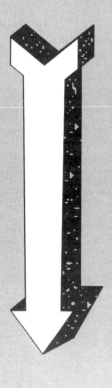

3. **Get Ready!** The best way to feel calm when the pressure is on is knowing that you've prepared properly. Ask yourself what you can do to get ready for your situation and what's in your control. Map out the things that you can do that will help. If you find yourself worrying about stuff that you can't control, repeat the words 'I can only do what I can do,' and focus on what you can change. For example, don't worry about what if you fail the test. Instead, get stuck into your revision and get a good night's rest so you're fresh and fired up for your test.

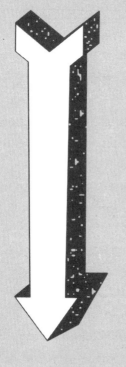

2. **Keep your brain balanced.** It is totally normal for your brain to imagine loads of different outcomes, but make sure you spend the same amount of time thinking about the *best* that could happen, as you spend thinking about the *worst* that could happen. Remember to also think about what is *most likely* to happen. Think back to times when you've been overly worried before or when you have faced a similar challenge and nailed it. Then remind yourself – you've done it before, and you can do it again. If you chose to take on a challenge, remembering **WHY** you wanted to give it a go can help you to keep going if you feel like giving up.

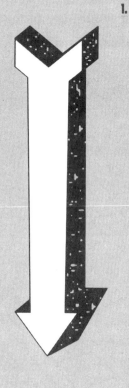

1. **Keep calm and carry on!** When you feel the pressure rising, the best thing you can do is relax your body. Close your eyes for a moment and release any tension you find in your hands, shoulders, forehead and jaw. Say something kind to yourself, such as 'I am going to give it my best shot, that's all I need to do.' Remind yourself that it's okay to have big emotions and that nerves and excitement feel really similar. Could this feeling just be anticipation and excitement? Take yourself off somewhere private and do a chicken wing or two (see page 23) or stay put and take five calming breaths to steady yourself (see page 44). You've got this!

STAMP OUT
FAMILY FEUDS

Our families see the best of us and the worst of us, and while we can't control other people's behaviour, we can take responsibility for our own.

Thankfully, there are lots of ways that you can help to keep things calm. Arguments are a natural part of being close to other people, but what's important is **HOW** you disagree and **WHAT** you do afterwards. So, if you've just stomped upstairs in a huff after a shouting match with your mum, or you lost it today with your brother, cut yourself some slack.

If someone's pushing your buttons, **KEEP YOUR COOL** in the heat of the moment by taking a pause. Take five long, slow breaths, count to ten, do whatever you need to do to step back, because lashing out will only make things worse. As calmly as you can, state clearly what's okay and what isn't in terms of how other people talk to you, treat you or use your belongings. You have every right to protect yourself, your time, your space and your stuff. You just need to communicate this carefully. Be clear about what has upset you. It's also totally okay to ask for the support of an adult you trust to help calm the situation.

Sometimes we need a time out to be able to fix a disagreement. If you're not getting anywhere, have a family code word that means 'time out' and an agreement from everyone to respect it when it's used. Take yourself off to calm down and resolve it when you are all in the right frame of mind. (Take a peek at page 159 for ideas.)

Every family argues and you shouldn't give yourself or your family a hard time over this. The quickest way to restore harmony is to say **SORRY** in a genuine, heartfelt way for any hurt you may have caused.

If someone else is offering to apologise and own their mistakes, be quick to accept the kind gesture. This will help you all to move more quickly back to a happy place.

As well as making up after family arguments, look out for the good stuff! When your brother or sister does something lovely, let them know straight away how happy it makes you. Let your parents or carers know about it so they can enjoy it, too. This helps your siblings feel good about themselves.

A little bit of **UNDERSTANDING** goes a long way, so listening to what's going on with your family members really helps and will make them feel cared for and supported. When you're aware of each other's problems, it is easier to be a little more patient and understanding.

SO, WHAT MAKES A GOOD APOLOGY?

A good apology is one that you really mean.

Show you mean it by acknowledging the mistake you made, taking responsibility for it and being clear that you regret the hurt you caused.

Don't ruin a good apology by throwing in words like 'but …' or 'because you …' You don't want to start a fresh argument!

We show we care by the words we use AND how we say them. When you're saying sorry, make eye contact, include kind gestures (such as offering a hug) and speak in soft tones.

Be kind to yourself, too. We all make mistakes, but it takes courage to own up to them and say sorry. What's done is done; put it down to experience. A good apology can actually bring your family closer together.

FIND YOUR INNER TREE

Let's get practical and make like a tree! This simple yoga pose will help you focus your attention and manage your emotions.

Your inner tree may sound and feel a little silly, but stick with me. It'll show you something **POWERFUL** about your mind. By understanding how your mind works, you are better able to focus it, which comes in handy when you're learning something new, tackling something tricky or squeezing the most joy out of a happy moment.

☆ Stand up, shake out your arms and legs and, as you do, imagine you are flicking away any heaviness. If you can, stand somewhere with a tree in your line of sight. If there's no trees, imagine one!

☆ Let calmness wash over you with your feet hip-width apart, and look at the tree in front of you. Bring the sole of your left foot to the inside of your right ankle, calf or higher up your leg if that feels good to you.

☆ You can hold your hands in front of your chest like you're praying, reach them up to the sky or, if you need to, stretch them out to the sides to help you balance. Don't worry if you wobble, this is all part of it.

☆ Stay here for five to ten slow, deep breaths, coming back into the pose if you lose your balance.

Notice how it's more difficult to balance when your mind wanders off. You probably feel calmer when you focus on the real or imaginary tree in front of you. Picture your roots going deep into the earth, the strength of your trunk and the lightness of your branches stretching towards the sky. When you're ready to release the pose, simply bring your foot back down to the ground and give your legs a shake out. Remember to try it on the other side. It may feel completely different!

When practising this pose, notice if you start to judge yourself on how successful you are at it. But remember, there's no right or wrong here, this is just a tree pose!

Use tree pose to help improve your focus. This can be helpful before you sit down to tackle something that needs your full attention. Come into your tree, and notice how it feels to be in this shape. Watch your mind dart about! It will wander, but **YOU** can choose where you direct your attention. We get better at focusing the more we practise.

DO NOTHING

Sometimes it is important to do absolutely nothing – we all need to be still at times! Relaxing your body will also help to soothe a busy mind.

Relaxing your body … sounds simple, right? But have you ever noticed how hard it can be to lie still? There's a secret trick that will help. This might sound a bit crazy, but to relax your body, you're going to tense it first.

Find a comfy space to lie down on your back with your arms and legs stretched out. Just notice how your body feels before you do anything else and, if you can, let your muscles relax. You might notice some **ZINGY** energy, and your body might not want to be still – that's okay! Now, start your squeezing exercises. Bend your arms, make fists and squeeze your arm muscles tightly.

Then let go. Notice how nice it feels to release the effort. Let's add to that first squeeze – bend your arms, make fists, squeeze your arm muscles **AND** lift your shoulders up to your ears. Then let it go. Now, add in another part – squeeze your hands, arms and shoulders to your ears, and shrivel your face up like a wrinkled raisin. And let it all go … it feels so good to let go of that squeeze! Add another area – tense your hands, arms, shoulders, face **AND** squeeze your tummy muscles. Then flop. One last part to add – squeeze your hands, arms, shoulders, face, tummy and tense your legs and toes, so your whole body is involved! And let it all go. Notice how comfortable it feels to be still now; how easy it is to relax your body. If it feels good to be lying down, stay for a while and enjoy the calm energy moving around your body.

If you're having a hard time falling asleep, this magic relaxation exercise can help you chill out and rest until sleep comes.

How can we use this trick to help us during the day? We can't always get down on the floor and do it, but we can also use parts of it anywhere, anytime. At your desk you could just do a little squeeze of your hands, or you could shrug your shoulders up to your ears and enjoy letting it go. Whenever you feel the pressure **RISING**, see what you can squeeze, and then soften it. This exercise will help you to feel calm and in control.

PLAN YOUR ATTACK

Is your mind feeling jumbled up? Have you got lots going on right now? Life (and our brains) can feel very busy at times.

It can be hard to know where to start when it comes to big projects, preparing for things such as school tests or just thinking about what you'll do in the holidays. Try a brain dump! Instead of mentally sifting through all your thoughts, thinking about all the things you have to get done and all the other stuff that you'd like to do, get them down on paper! Just remembering them all is a job in itself. Writing them all down will free up your brain power.

You could write down each of your thoughts in a little bubble, or you could make each one the spoke of a giant wheel, whatever you feel like. The act of writing will help you identify the things that are important to you and the things that need your attention right away. Once you see it all on paper, you can more easily cross out the stuff you don't really need to do. Enjoy crossing things out and freeing up that energy!

You can highlight or colour in the things that you need to tackle. Try using a traffic-light code – red for 'right away', amber for 'next on the list' and green for 'if I have time'. Seeing it all mapped out in one place will help you form a plan. It can also relax your brain, knowing that when your list is on paper, you don't have to keep holding it all in your head.

Next, take the things in red that need to be done first and break them down into small steps if they feel overwhelming. Come back to your list when you've finished a task and enjoy crossing them off and giving yourself a pat on the back for a job well done.

Use this strategy whenever your mind is feeling full, and you'll be able to see a clearer picture of where to begin. One step at a time.

STAND LIKE A WARRIOR

Did you know that how you sit and stand affects how you feel? Don't take my word for it. See for yourself!

Psychologist Erik Peper has been doing some interesting research into how we use our bodies and his findings are really clear: the quickest way to shift your mood is to change your posture.

RESEARCH ROUND-UP

✳ A TALL, UPRIGHT POSTURE WILL LIFT YOUR MOOD
   AND ENERGY LEVELS COMPARED TO A SLUMPED
   POSTURE, WHICH LOWERS YOUR MOOD AND ENERGY.

✳ YOU'RE MORE LIKELY TO REMEMBER NEGATIVE
   MEMORIES WHEN YOU'RE SLOUCHING COMPARED
   TO WHEN YOU'RE UPRIGHT.

✳ SITTING TALL RATHER THAN SLOUCHING CAN IMPROVE
   MATHS PERFORMANCE AND REDUCE TEST ANXIETY!

STAND UP FOR YOURSELF

We all know what a slump looks like … so whenever you notice yourself sinking, make a change! To feel energised and ready for your day, lengthen your spine, broaden your chest and look straight ahead. Even better than reminding yourself about this posture, let's build the muscles that hold you in this shape – you need strong tummy and back muscles. Take a **WARRIOR POSE** every day. This powerful yoga posture fires up those very body parts!

1. This yoga pose is called Warrior 1. Stand with your feet hip-width apart, as if you're standing on train tracks. Lunge forwards with your right foot, staying on those train tracks.

2. Bend your front knee deeply and press your back heel towards the floor (it won't touch, but you'll feel a lovely stretch in your back calf). Breathe in and raise your arms up (making a 'V' shape) with your palms facing each other. As you breathe out, bring your elbows down so that your arms make a 'W' shape.

3. Repeat this six to ten times, feeling it strengthen your back, open your chest and work your tummy and legs. When you've finished, shake out your legs and repeat the sequence with your left foot forwards. Make like a warrior every day and notice how strong it makes you feel – in mind and body!

FLIP YOUR THINKING

There are phrases we can use to feel more powerful. Try these ones out for size!

INSTEAD OF 'I HAVE TO' ...

Why not switch it up for '**I GET TO**'? Saying 'I have to go to football' or 'I have to go to school' can make you feel pushed around by the words 'I have to'. But if you switch them for 'I get to', you realise that someone else might **LOVE** the things that you were thinking of as a chore. It might just plant a seed of gratitude (see page 41).

INSTEAD OF 'WHYS' AND 'WHAT IFS' ...

Try breaking the pattern by asking 'What can *I* do?' It's easy for your brain to get stuck on a bunch of **WHYS** and **WHAT IFS**. *Why* did my friend say that unkind comment to me? *What if* she's angry with me? *What if* I don't understand the questions in my maths test? Break the loop by focusing on what **YOU** can do. We can't control what our friends say or feel, and we don't write the maths tests, but there are lots of things we **CAN** do to make ourselves feel better.

For example, you could talk to your friend and find out why they said what they did, rather than just wonder and worry. These steps help you feel more in control of the situation.

INSTEAD OF 'I CAN'T' ...

How about swapping '**I CAN'T**' for '**I DON'T**'? The words 'I can't' can make you feel bossed around, but 'I don't' puts you in charge. Are your friends pestering you about replying to messages at night? Try saying, 'I don't use my phone after 7.30 p.m.' Does it feel more powerful? If your mates are doing something you don't agree with, saying 'I don't' means you own it, but 'I can't' sounds like someone else is setting the rules. You choose what's right for you.

Maybe there's something that makes you feel a bit resentful? 'I don't' watch screens in the hour before bed feels much more like it's something you are in control of. It doesn't have anything to do with what you're allowed to do. Saying 'I don't' makes it about the choices **YOU** are making.

GET **TOUCHY**

Feeling low? Listen to that urge to HUG IT OUT! There is nothing like a cuddle to soothe the soul, after all.

Cuddling doesn't just feel nice, it actually changes your brain chemistry! When we're wrapped up in a cuddle our brains release a hormone called oxytocin. This is the hormone that helps mothers and babies to bond, and it's something we rely on our whole lives. Human beings have a need to belong and feel loved, just as much as we need food in our bellies. Touch, thanks to the effects of oxytocin, is a powerful way to help us feel safe and calm. Think of it as a feel-good medicine.

When you're feeling wobbly, how can you get the oxytocin flowing to help you calm down? Try a loving hug with a family member or a friend, curling up with your dog or cat or a soak in the bath. Wrapping your hands around a warm mug of milk or nuzzling into a **SOFT** blanket can help, too. Look out for ways you can harness the power of touch and jot them down in your journal.

BANISH THE COBWEBS

You might think you're not bothered by mess, but have you noticed how much calmer you feel when your room is neat and tidy?

Your environment has a big impact on how you feel – your energy, your ability to think straight and to feel relaxed. It can even have an impact on your sleep. Take a good look at your bedroom and think about how it could be affecting you. A simple spot of tidying and organising can blow away the cobwebs in your mind. Get rid of dust and you can breathe easier. A houseplant can do wonders for making your room feel like a calm, safe place and you might really enjoy having something of your own to look after.

Maybe something needs a big sort-out? Your drawers, wardrobe, desk, books, games or those storage boxes under your bed that have been there for ages? It doesn't matter where you start, just choose one thing to tackle, listen to your favourite music and get stuck in. You might unearth some **TREASURES** while you're it.

Create a memory box to keep photos of special things you find. It's not the physical stuff that brings you joy, it's the memories.

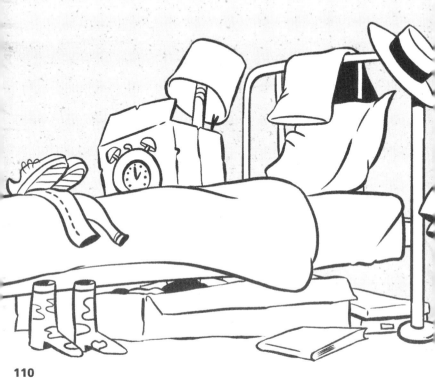

Think of ways that your clear-out can become an act of kindness for someone else. What can you give to others? Can you make someone happy with hand-me-downs, donate to charity or swap some clothes you no longer wear with friends? Are there things you can sell, upcycle or recycle?

Have a good clean-up and see how having things in order on the outside makes you feel more **CALM** on the inside. You can go beyond your bedroom too. Lend a hand to keep things neat around the house and you'll make everyone happy!

SPRAY FOR YOUR SANITY

Imagine for a moment the smell of freshly cut grass, cupcakes baking in the oven, salty sea air, juicy oranges at half time, the comfort of your mum's perfume or dad's aftershave, pine needles in the woods …

Scent has the amazing ability to bring back powerful memories that can make us feel happy. Not only that, different scents can make us experience all kinds of different emotions, too.

We can draw on the power of scent using essential oils (extracts from plants that capture their fragrance). Some scents – such as jasmine and citrus – can energise and uplift us. These ones can get us going in the morning. Others, such as peppermint, rosemary and cinnamon, help us concentrate and can boost memory, which is really useful when we're sitting down to get work done. Some scents, such as vanilla, rose and lavender, calm and soothe us. They are perfect for bedtime or whenever you want to chill out.

SCENTS TO MAKE YOU FEEL BETTER

☆ What are some of your favourite smells and why? Be on the lookout for these in your day and seize the opportunity to 'smell the roses'.

☆ With the help of a grown-up, make your own spray for bedtime. Find a clean spray bottle, partially fill it with water, put on protective gloves and add a few drops of a soothing essential oil. Then make your own label – 'happy dreams', 'happy sleep' or 'a spray to scare any monsters away'! Spray your pillow for a peaceful sleep.

☆ Create your own all-natural roll-on. Grab a grown-up and work together. You'll need a small, empty glass roll-on bottle (a 10 ml bottle is perfect). Wearing protective gloves, add almond oil or grapeseed oil and 5–10 drops of an essential oil that you love (make sure it's safe to use on skin and won't cause irritation). Pop in the rollerball, screw on the cap, give it a good shake and you've got a little dose of happiness in your pocket. Swipe it over your wrists, rub them together and let the smell lift you up.

If you don't have essential oils at home, you can explore what's available in the garden or a park. Look for rose petals, honeysuckle and lavender, or experiment with herbs like basil. Place the petals or leaves into a bowl, add half a cup of water, stir it with a spoon and squeeze the plants with your fingers. Using a strainer to catch the petals, pour the liquid into a clean spray bottle. Pop on the spray nozzle and you have your very own homemade perfume. For more intense fragrance you can leave the petals to soak overnight or for a few hours in the sunshine.

If you're feeling stressed, or finding it hard to focus or get to sleep, remember that scent is part of your awesome happiness toolkit!

DETOX YOUR DEVICES

Technology is big part of life, helping us to learn, have fun and stay connected with people – but it's important to get the BALANCE right.

Technology is there to help you. You don't have to be a slave to it and let screens get you down! Technology can suck us in and keep us wanting more. It's very stimulating for our brains and it can leave us wired and stressed out. Even adults can have a hard time knowing when it's time to step away from their devices. Think about your posture when you're in front of a screen, too – it's easy to slump, which sends our mood on a downwards spiral (see page 99).

10 TIPS FOR TECH HEALTH

1. Screens can be a great way to connect with other people. They allow us to stay up-to-date with their news and let them know that we care. But they can also be a massive distraction. Knowing when to put your phone down is important. Suggest a phone-free zone at the dinner table to encourage everyone to chat.

2. Tech time doesn't have to be alone time. Video calls are a great way to keep in touch with people, or you can check in with a mate by messaging or gaming together. There are lots of options!

3. Agree some technology rules with your parents or carers and siblings, so that you all follow the same rules. Maybe you could leave all your devices out of sight in one place, because just the sight of one can get your brain firing and your hand itching to pick it up. Enjoy mealtimes without screens, and if you all decide to sit down and watch a film together, leave all the distractions in another room.

4. Make sure your tech use doesn't eat into time for other ways of having fun. Set aside *at least* an hour every day after school to have tech-free fun. This could include face-to-face conversations, exercise or spending time in nature. We need variety in our downtime to feel our best.

5. Notice the effect that your device is having on your mood and your thinking. If it is making you feel down or you're comparing yourself to others you see on social media or TV, it's time to take a break. Try some mood-boosting activities instead (see page 63).

6. Sit up! Don't hunch over your device. Get into an upright posture. Slouching creates tension in your neck and shoulders.

7. Get a good dose of natural light, instead of your phone's artificial light, in the morning to boost your body clock. This helps you get better quality sleep.

8. Commit to at least 60 minutes of screen-free time before you go to bed. The blue light emitted from screens disrupts the body's production of melatonin, the sleep hormone we need to help us drop off with ease.

9. When you go to bed, put your phone to bed, too – somewhere other than your bedroom. That way you won't be tempted to pick it up, which will ping your brain into action when you should be resting. Use a traditional alarm clock rather than your phone.

10. Be aware of how long you spend on your device each day. Use an app to set a time limit for social media, messaging and games on your devices. That way, you know when enough is enough, and when to go and do something else that's screen-free.

A PEAR-SHAPED PLAN

Things can go wrong. Sometimes we have a brain fade, we make a poor choice or say the wrong thing. Occasionally we might lash out, or fall out with friends or family. Despite good intentions, well-made plans and preparations, things don't always go as we'd hoped. What can we do when things go wrong?

We can talk …

We've all felt bad about something we've done (or not done), and we've all been on the receiving end of unpleasant behaviour, too. You don't have to face these bad feelings on your own. Draw on the support of the people who love you, and know that you can do a bad thing without being a bad person. Equally, if someone has been unkind to you, remember it is not your fault and you do not deserve it.

In addition to the love of people in your corner, make a plan for when things go pear-shaped to help you feel better!

COUNTDOWN TO GETTING BACK ON TRACK

5. Beating yourself up doesn't change what's happened, it just makes you feel worse. It can make it harder to apologise and make amends, too. So be kind to yourself. If you've made a mistake, as well as putting things right and seeking forgiveness, you need to forgive yourself, too.

4. Step up and say you're sorry. (See page 86 for how to make a good apology.) You need to be brave and own anything that you are responsible for. Taking responsibility for your behaviour will help you avoid repeating past mistakes. It's good to try and recognise when circumstances were beyond your control, too.

3. Look for the lesson. What has this experience taught you? Has it shown you what is really important to you, such as loyalty, trustworthiness, kindness, honesty, courage or fairness? What might you do differently next time? Remember: it's always okay to ask for help when you're finding things hard.

2. What do **YOU** need to do to feel better? What will help you
    shake this off? Do you want to write a letter to say sorry, ask
    for help or write a journal entry to get things off your chest?
    Or maybe all you need is a simple distraction?

1. One of the most powerful ways we can help ourselves feel
    better is by talking to ourselves with care. Talk to yourself like
    you would your best friend. You know that voice you have in
    your head that reviews what you said or did, and that comments
    on what you might do in the future? Sometimes this voice can
    become super-nasty.

If your 'inner critic' is saying something unkind, remember it is just a thought and tell it to buzz off! Replace it with something you would say to a friend instead.

Try this: imagine in your mind you have a whole bunch of voices. As well as the inner critic, there's a **CHEERLEADER**, a friendly voice, maybe one that is like a kind and wise grandparent. They all have something to say to you. You can choose to pass the mic to the voice that makes you feel bad, or you can let the voice that cheers you on have the mic!

CELEBRATE YOU!

We all have tricky days where things don't go as planned. But make sure you notice the good stuff you achieved, too!

Even on rubbish days, you will find a little glimmer that was okay. Grab your journal or find a comfy place to just lie back and bask in the warm glow of what went well, or what you achieved, even in the middle of a bad day.

If you want to get an even bigger feel-good boost, think about *why* those things happened. Maybe you had a lovely afternoon with your friend after a stressful morning. Why? Because you care about each other and have the same idea of what's fun. Or, you kept calm in the middle of a difficult quiz. Why? Because even though it was challenging, you had worked hard and gave it your best shot. Feel how the 'why' boosts a positive mood.

If you've been working on a challenge (see page 37), you don't have to save the happy dance just for the end result. Recognise the mini milestones and celebrate the efforts you are making along the way. And of course, enjoy the achievement of finally checking off that goal before you even think about what's next!

If you're enjoying thinking about this stuff, you could jot down things you've achieved in your journal each day or once a week. Make a note of the times you've been brave or the new things you've tried. The powerful thing about writing down these achievements is that you can return to your journal when things get tough and be reminded of your courage and strength. You've done it before, and you can do it again!

TURN UP THE VOLUME

Want to flip your feelings? Music can switch things up in an instant! Do some planning so that you have music for every mood at your fingertips.

Different types of music or even individual songs can have different effects on our mood. Identify your favourite tunes to lift your spirits, help you focus and calm you down. Build a playlist for each one.

For example, if you need energising in the morning, make a playlist of your favourite dance tracks. If you feel angry or stressed, choose rock music to let it all out, or the sound of nature (such as the ocean or rainfall) to calm you down. Try turning to classical music for motivation and focus (remember this one the next time you're studying).

There is nothing like music to help you work through
your feelings, no matter what they are!

GET CRAFTY

Feeling in a bad mood and don't know how to get out of it? Looking for a pressure release after a school day? Bust out of a bad mood with creativity!

Sometimes, all we need to feel better is a bit of **FREEDOM** and **FUN** – a place where there are no rules, no right or wrong, no good or bad; where there doesn't have to be a goal or even an outcome!

Getting creative gives you a chance to express yourself. It can help you cope with your feelings, or it can just be a happy distraction. It's also a great way to engage your brain in different ways and can improve your problem-solving skills, confidence, patience and determination.

There are so many ways to unleash your creative spirit. Think outside the art and craft box! You could …

Doodle, draw, paint, collage, colour in, make a flip book cartoon, design an outfit, get out the **face paint**, make some **origami** or fortune tellers, build a model, invent something, write a story, **write a poem**, write a song, sing, **play an instrument**, bake, create a website, make your own **animation** on "Scratch", do some **coding**, take some photos, or make a film on iMovie. Still stuck for inspiration? Leap over to 5-Minute Crafts PLAY on YouTube and you'll find something cool to try.

Forget the idea that what you create needs to be something special. It's just about enjoying the process. Let loose! There's no pressure here, express yourself and have fun. What you create is totally up to you.

MEET YOUR BELLY BRAIN

Sometimes when you have a poorly tummy you might also find yourself feeling down in the dumps. But why?

Did you know that your gut health and your mental health are linked? Knowing this fact might help you understand why you feel blue or irritable when you have a tummy upset.

About 100 trillion microorganisms live in your digestive system, including at least 1,000 different types of bacteria. Not all bacteria are bad for us. Some are essential, helping your body digest food and fight infections. Some gut bacteria produce chemicals that your brain uses for learning, memory and mood. In fact, about 95 per cent of the body's supply of serotonin (the hormone that helps keep you happy and calm) is produced in the gut by bacteria!

Be gentle on yourself if you're recovering from a bout of illness. When gut bacteria gets thrown out of whack after taking antibiotics or because of a virus, your mood can be affected.

You won't feel like this for long, though. Make make sure you're getting plenty of fresh fruits and vegetables. These are all packed with fibre that promote the growth of good bacteria. An apple is a good choice (wash it and keep the skin on). Other healthy options include live yoghurt, almonds, blueberries, bananas, green peas, broccoli, garlic and olive oil drizzled over cooked veggies. You could even get adventurous and try Japanese miso soup or Korean kimchi!

FLASH YOUR GNASHERS

When you feel a little grouchy, it can be hard to turn your mood around. Try a smile and see if it helps to lighten the load.

When you smile, your body cleverly releases the feel-good hormones dopamine and serotonin. They boost your happiness and make your heart beat more slowly to calm you down.

A **SMILE** tells your brain you are happy, and a fake smile has the same effect as a real one. So you can trick your body into giving you a dose of happy hormones. Fake it 'til you make it!

There are two main muscles in your face that help you smile: zygomaticus major, the muscle that draws the corners of your lips outwards and upwards, and the orbicularis oculi, the eye crinkler. Say hello to them whenever you feel a bit down, and put them to work with a big smile. Hold it for for 10–15 seconds, and make sure you smile with your whole face.

Even better, try smiling at someone else and see if they smile back. Smiles tend to be contagious. While your body can't tell the difference between a real and a fake smile, people can, so make sure you flex your orbicularis oculi muscles!

BE SOMEONE'S HERO

When you're feeling down, it's easy to get stuck on thinking about what YOU need. Shake it up by thinking about who needs you.

Helping other people is a sure-fire way to feel connected, and it will get you feeling positive about yourself. It feels good to be kind, and you'll get a huge surge of energy from it, too. But remember, the main focus should always be about doing a good turn, not just making yourself feel good.

Have a think about the people around you – who could do with a **HELPING HAND**? Could you help make dinner or take the dog for a walk? Do you have a neighbour who might like some company? Is there a friend who needs a bit of cheering up? Notice how much your brother or sister loves it when you involve them in your games.

Go beyond the people you know and see if you can sprinkle some **KINDNESS** around to those you don't. Offer a smile, pay a heart-felt compliment, say thanks for someone else's hard work, hold a door open or take care of the environment by picking up litter.

There are so many ways to be someone's hero. When you have performed a kind act, write about it in your journal. Jot down what you did, how the other person reacted and how it made you feel. Enjoy the energy and positivity you've created and notice how it boosts your own self-esteem. Everyone deserves kindness and we all have a part to play. Notice how reading back your entries helps you experience the same warm glow all over again. Who needs **YOU** today?

FRIENDS vs FRENEMIES

We need our friends almost as much as we need air to breathe. But what makes a good friend?

Sometimes friendship can be confusing. People can be kind one day and ignore us the next. Being clear on what you value in a friendship can be very useful in sorting out the friends from the frenemies.

SO, WHAT MAKES A GOOD MATE AND HOW CAN YOU BE ONE, TOO?

✓ Good friends bring out the best in you. They say and do kind things, they're happy for you when good stuff happens in your life and they're there for you when you need support.

✓ Sometimes it's your love of a common interest that brings you together, but you don't have to have everything in common. Good friends will celebrate your differences too, giving you space to be you and liking you for who you are.

✓ You know you can trust your good friends with your secrets.

✓ If you have a disagreement, good friends will let you know when you've upset them. When you let them know they've hurt your feelings, a good friend will apologise and try not to make the same mistake again.

✓ Good friendships are balanced. This is where you both have a turn making decisions, you both have a chance to talk and you both make sure you take the time to listen.

✓ Bear in mind that everyone has off days, even your best friends will get it wrong sometimes. We all make mistakes, so good friends will cut each other some slack at times.

Be on the lookout for FRENEMIES! Sometimes people seem to be your friend, but their behaviour towards you can change from kind to unkind with seemingly little reason. Perhaps this person isn't someone to depend upon.

✗ Frenemies are not loyal. They might share your secrets or talk about you behind your back.

✗ They might put limits on your friendship or pressure you to do things you don't want to do, saying you can be friends only if you do what they tell you.

✗ Frenemies sometimes let you join in, but leave you out at other times.

✗ They say mean things or laugh at you.

✗ Frenemies have a talent for making you feel bad about yourself.

If someone is being unkind to you, remember it is not your fault, and it's not you who needs to change. No one has the right to hurt you or pressure you to do anything. You can try to talk to them about their behaviour and explain how it makes you feel. It's possible they didn't realise, so give them a chance to step up and be a good friend.

If they **APOLOGISE**, it shows you they care. If they blame you or shrug it off, you know this isn't someone to choose to be around. It can be sad and scary to move on from a friendship, but remember, you always deserve to be treated with kindness.

Know your true friends and choose to spend time with them. And if you find you're wanting to make some new friends, joining clubs or getting involved in activities you love is a great way to meet new people. Don't wait to be asked, invite others to join you!

NATURE ROCKS!

Something getting you down? Turn to Mother Nature – she will have some wisdom for you. Watching nature as it grows and changes reminds you that, just like stormy weather, tough times won't last for ever.

Look out for reassuring signs in your garden or local park: there is **BEAUTY** in the bloom of a flower and nourishment in petals as they brown, fall and return to the earth to feed the soil. Beginnings and endings are normal, a natural part of life and every life cycle and season is important. See how determined nature is – tiny flowers will grow up through cracks in the pavement and weeping willow will bend, not break, with the wind – and know that we can be just as resilient.

Soaking up the beauty around you both **RELAXES** and **ENERGISES** you. Unplug from technology, stop rushing around and get a dose of nature. Being in nature builds your curiosity, mindfulness and appreciation of the world around you. All of these help make you happy. Given that nature is all around you, all you need to do is check in and you'll feel better for it.

10 WAYS TO HANG OUT WITH MOTHER NATURE

1. Get up early and take in a sunrise or try star gazing at night.

2. Get your hands in the mud or bare feet on the grass.

3. Plant your own seeds and watch them grow.

4. Search for minibeasts and observe them at work.

5. Watch the clouds and trees moving in the breeze or look for birds flying by.

6. Try pond or rock-pool dipping, skim some stones or just watch the waves.

7. Count all the different shapes of leaves you can find.

8. Search for four-leaf clovers.

9. Make nature collages or create a pattern of pinecones or shells.

10. Feed the local birds or walk your dog (or a neighbour's dog).

BANK YOUR MEMORIES

Want to put a smile on your face? Then learn how to savour!

Don't worry if you haven't heard of savouring before, because you are already a **MASTER** at it. Savouring is the ability to pay attention to pleasurable experiences, where you truly feel every sensation. Think of that square of chocolate you enjoyed like it was the last bit of chocolate in the world. Remember that rainbow that stopped you in your tracks? Think of that hug that filled you with happiness from head to toe. Focusing on each of these things as they happen is savouring! By paying careful attention, you can more easily come back to each happy memory and relish the emotion you felt at that time.

THREE WAYS TO SAVOUR THE GOOD STUFF

1. **SAVOUR THE PAST:** SPEND TIME THINKING ABOUT SOMETHING HAPPY THAT'S ALREADY HAPPENED

2. **SAVOUR THE PRESENT:** USE YOUR MINDFULNESS MUSCLES (SEE PAGE 63) RIGHT NOW

3. **SAVOUR THE FUTURE:** LOOK FORWARD TO SOMETHING EXCITING COMING UP

Just knowing about the skill of savouring will help you pay attention to the happy things in life. With the skill of savouring under your belt you'll never let a happy moment pass you by unnoticed, and you can come back to that feeling anytime you're feeling unhappy. That's another superpower right there!

FIND YOUR MISSION STATEMENT

Want to know the secret to a long and happy life? Look no further than the people from the Japanese island of Okinawa.

In Okinawa there are more centenarians than anywhere else in the world – that's people who have reached 100 years old! People from Okinawa can expect to live a whole ten years longer than people in other parts of the world, such as the UK or USA. What's their secret? It's not just a diet rich in fish and vegetables, it's something they call **IKIGAI**!

Ikigai (pronounced eeky-guy) can be translated as 'a reason for being'. You can harness the power of ikigai by thinking about what's important to you and looking for ways that you can make a difference to the world. Remember when we found our superpower (see page 64)? Scroll through your strengths and think about what you want to change in the world. Take action and feel how that sense of purpose lifts you up.

Anyone can step up and create change, when they put their minds to it. Lots of young people are making a big difference. Greta Thunberg has become a leading voice for climate-change activism. At just 11 years old, Malala Yousafzai began an anonymous blog about her life under the Taliban rule in Pakistan. In 2014, aged 17, she became the youngest person to win the Nobel Peace Prize for her work to improve education for girls. After helping a blind woman cross the road, 12-year-old Alex Deans created iAid, a navigation device to guide blind people. All proof that you can make a contribution to the world at any age.

What are you passionate about? Write down what steps you can take to create your own **RIPPLES OF CHANGE**. These could be in your home, your street, your neighbourhood or at your school. Even the tiniest action can snowball into something powerful.

STRIKE A
POSE

Get ready for a power pose! Try this simple and fun yoga sequence and feel your confidence grow.

Start with some **MOUNTAIN BREATHS**. Stand up tall with your feet hip-width apart and arms down by your sides. Take a deep breath in through your nose, raising your arms out to the sides and up above your head. Look up and feel your mood lift up, too. As you breathe out through your nose, slowly lower your arms back down and look forwards. Stretch all the way to your fingertips, and don't flop or slouch. Take six of these assertive breaths and feel confident and powerful!

Next, channel your inner warrior with a pose called **WARRIOR 2**. Hold your arms out at shoulder height, and place your feet wide apart, roughly underneath your wrists. Turn your right foot so it faces the same direction as your right hand. Next, wriggle your left heel away from you a little, so it is on a diagonal angle, and press the outer edge of your left foot firmly into the floor. Bend your right knee deeply and keep your back leg super-straight.

Reach through your arms, palms facing downwards. Look towards your right hand. You should look like a surfer riding an enormous wave. Recognise how strong your legs are and feel the muscles that run up and down your spine, holding you there. Take five breaths in this powerful shape, knowing that you can stand up for yourself. Give your legs a shake and repeat the pose on the other side.

Practise these poses often. Whenever you need to draw on some extra **STRENGTH** during your day, think back to how powerful and strong they made you feel. Try to harness that sense of power to deal with anything your day throws at you.

MEET YOUR RAGE

No one likes to feel angry, but it's something everyone experiences now and again. Finding ways to manage it wisely is key.

Anger is a totally normal emotion. It helps us step up and speak out, so we don't want to get rid of it entirely. But we do need to learn how to manage our anger, so we don't do and say things that cause harm or upset. You can learn how to feel and express anger without lashing out.

We can feel angry for all sorts of reasons. Spending a lot of time on screens, being hungry or tired, or having to do things that we don't like can all fuel our anger. Getting fired up in these circumstances doesn't solve any problems! By getting a handle on your anger, you can stop the 'stress response' from kicking in, which makes it hard to think straight. To do this, you need a plan!

INTRODUCING YOUR KEEP-CALM PLAN

☆ **Take time out to simmer down.** If you can, take yourself off to a quiet space and wait until your emotions pass. If you have to stay put, you can still step back from the situation by counting to ten or practising your **TAKE FIVE** exercise (see page 46).

☆ **Name your feelings.** Sometimes, when it's difficult to identify your feelings, they can erupt as anger. Dig around and find out what's underneath them. Ask yourself, **WHY** did I react that way? Anger can also be a symptom of frustration, upset, irritation, fear, confusion, resentment, disappointment, hurt and worry. You can experience several of these feelings all at once, so see if pinpointing them helps you better understand what is going on and why. Notice how getting curious with your own emotions can help change your reactions.

☆ **Relax your body**. It's really hard to stay angry when you relax your muscles. Notice how your posture changes when you're angry: squeezed fists, a tight tummy or a clenched jaw. Breathe deeply and relax the muscles of your face (especially your eyes and jaw), drop your shoulders away from your ears, let your hands go floppy and breathe into your tummy.

☆ **Breathe out slowly.** Making your out breath longer than your in breath can be really soothing. You can also use your exhale to focus and calm yourself, instead of saying hurtful things. Try a '**LION BREATH**' to roar it out: breathe in through your nose, then exhale through your mouth while sticking your tongue as far out as possible, making a powerful 'HAAA' sound. Three breaths ought to do it.

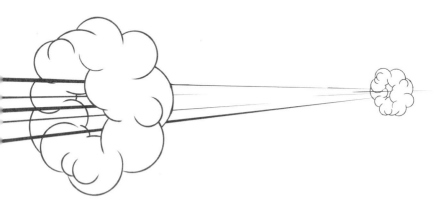

☆ **Get it all out!** Let it go on a piece of paper, sing a happy song or scream into a pillow. All of these methods help you get rid of the energetic charge of anger.

☆ **Think it through.** Lastly, once you have calmed down, ask yourself what your anger was trying to tell you. Has it shown you something important? Is there anything you need to do now to set things straight? Now that you're calm, it's time to take thoughtful action to look after yourself and other people.

GET **CURIOUS**

Next time things feel like they are going wrong, or not going to plan, take some time out to investigate why. Don't get mad, get curious!

When things don't turn out as you'd hoped, it's easy to feel grumpy or blame other people. And when someone upsets you, it's natural to leap to conclusions. Sometimes we decide they did something out of spite and that usually makes us feel worse.

Just like gratitude and kindness, curiosity is a skill that has serious **POWER** to change your perspective and lift you up. Okay, so this thing has happened, but let's think of three reasons why, rather than getting attached to just one. If someone was unkind towards you, what are some different explanations for their behaviour? If you did badly on that test, rather than get angry, think about why and what you can learn from the situation. Get curious about how you could react differently next time. Has everything really gone wrong, or is it just a small setback? What other parts of life are actually just fine?

It's surprisingly easy to build the **CURIOSITY** habit. When you're feeling stuck, try using the words 'I WONDER …'. **I WONDER** what else I could try to solve this problem? **I WONDER** what would happen if I tried something new, such as asking a friend to help me study a tricky subject? **I WONDER** why I'm feeling uneasy right now? Am I tired or hangry; is there something I've forgotten to do, or do I just need a hug?

Curiosity can also help you understand other people, allowing you to put yourself in their shoes. You could consider questions such as: I wonder if they might have had a bad day, or I wonder how that person might be feeling to make them say that?

Curiosity can go beyond questioning emotions and reactions. If there's something that baffles you, such as how things work or what a word means, get into the habit of asking questions and doing some fact finding. What do you find **FASCINATING**? Look into it, and find out more. Seek out a documentary or book on something new to you. When you're curious you engage your sense of awe and wonder about the world. Feel how this is both an inspiring use of your free time and how curiosity helps you manage tricky moments in life.

CANCEL
COMPARISONS

It is natural to notice other people, but comparing yourself to them, especially if you feel they have more than you, is a sure-fire recipe for misery.

Don't let the green-eyed monster get you down! Remember that everyone has insecurities, strengths and weaknesses. You might be jealous of someone else or what they have, but there will also be things that you have or can do that other people will be envious of. Every time your thoughts are drawn to what others have, bring your mind back to what you do have and celebrate **YOU**! Think your legs are the wrong shape, or not fast enough? Thank them for the thousands of miles they've carried you. Wish you had someone else's packed lunch? Remember how fortunate you are. Some kids have to walk several kilometres every day just to find safe drinking water.

It can be easy to live in a bubble of privilege and not take the time to see how fortunate we are. Appreciate the things that you do have and be mindful of those who have less. Stay grounded in gratitude to stay happy.

If it looks like someone has it all, consider the idea that it might not actually be true. Don't compare how you feel inside to how others look on the outside. You never know the struggles other people are facing behind the smiles. Everyone has **CHALLENGES** in life, no one has it all sorted! We're all muddling our way through, doing the best that we can.

Try to remember that what you see on social media, TV, in commercials, films and magazines has been made to **LOOK** perfect. In other words, don't believe everything you see. Comparing yourself to others can be a bad habit. See it for the downer it is and exchange it for something that makes you feel more positive about yourself.

A LIBRARY FOR HAPPY DOWNTIME

How you spend your free time can make a huge difference to your happiness – so choose wisely!

What you read, watch, play and listen to can make you feel great or it can really get you down. Not all downtime is equal! Choose to spend your time on things that give you energy and help you feel happy. Have you noticed how some shows make you feel worried or upset, or how some games make you feel jittery afterwards? If what you are taking in through your eyes and ears brings you down or makes it hard to sleep, choose something else! If you feel affected by what other people are watching or listening to at home, it's okay to let them know.

Identify **POSITIVE** ways to chill out. Make your own list of books, magazines, websites, films, games, podcasts and TV shows that make you feel calm or good about yourself and the world. Be inspired by your friends, and ask them about the things that they are enjoying. If you feel worried, or whenever you've got a moment to yourself, turn to your list and choose what to do carefully. Just like we need lots of different kinds and colours of fruits and vegetables in our diet to stay healthy, we need a variety of nice things to do in our free time.

SEARCH OUT SOMEWHERE SPECIAL

Need a place to relax and calm down? Seek out a cosy corner or a spot in nature to unwind.

Have you got a happy place? Is it snuggled up in bed, surrounded by your favourite things? Is it an armchair by the window where you can look out and see the trees moving in the breeze? Or is it running along a beach with the sun warming your skin?

If your safe place is indoors, make it **COSY**. Fill it with things you love the feel and colour of – your favourite pillows, cushions, rugs or blankets – and photographs of happy memories. Burrow down deep and feel comforted. This is your calm, safe place that you can come to whenever you feel worried.

You can also find places in nature that give you a sense of security and **CALM**. Being by still water can feel calming, whereas moving water or crashing waves can feel exciting. Being up high with a far-reaching view can feel freeing and awe inspiring. Walking in open fields can help clear your mind. Just feeling your bare feet on the grass can feel reassuring. Where is your safe place in nature?

If it's not possible to visit your safe place, close your eyes and go to these places in your mind. Imagine being there, feeling the powerful effects on your mind and body. You could write about journeys to the places you love. Or come up with an imaginary place that brings you calm. Do you like to go alone or does someone else go with you? What creatures might you find along the way? What might you do and see there? Be as descriptive as you can, using all your senses. With the power of your imagination, you can go there any time and feel the benefits.

SPEAK UP

A valuable tool in our happiness kit is knowing when to speak up with confidence and stand up for ourselves. You've got this.

It's not always easy or comfortable, but if someone is doing something that upsets you, you need to let them know, otherwise nothing will change. Maybe they're saying something about you that's not true or using a nickname that you don't like. At times like these, we need to use our voices and ask them to stop. We also need the courage to ask questions when we don't understand.

Speaking up is a strength we can call upon when we're trying to get our point across. This takes a special kind of confidence called assertiveness, and it is something we can all learn.

Being assertive allows you to tell other people what you feel is right and fair. It's not enough to just think it (people are not mind readers!). Let your voice be heard. Sometimes people don't realise that what they're doing is causing upset and that's where assertiveness is really helpful.

Assertiveness is all about self-respect. It's not being difficult or bossy, it is just a way to keep yourself safe and healthy. It is a skill that uses your voice, posture, eye contact and choice of words. You can stand tall, just as you did with your mountain breaths (see page 156), and say in a loud, clear voice: 'Stop, I don't like it. That's not okay.' You could raise your hand in a **STOP** sign. Look directly into a person's eyes to show them that you mean what you say. There are no apologies needed here. You have every right to calmly and confidently say 'No.'

This can take some **PRACTICE**, so when you're doing your warrior 1 yoga pose (see page 101), you can add your courageous eye contact and your assertive voice to the exercise. You can practise this in the mirror or brainstorm some different ways of saying what's okay and what's not okay with a trusted friend, carer or family member. Remember, assertiveness is a muscle you build with practice, and it's okay if it feels difficult at first. Being assertive is how we show the world we respect ourselves and other people and it's how we build happy, healthy relationships.

REBOOT YOURSELF

Simple yoga stretches are a great way to recharge both body and mind.

Just like your phone or computer, you need to recharge! You can use your body to calm yourself after an argument, or before a test. These yoga poses are perfect before bed, too, helping you soothe away sadness and worry.

3 EASY WAYS TO RECHARGE

1. **All-fours warm-up.** Come down onto your hands and knees. Place your knees underneath your hips, your hands under your shoulders and spread your fingers out wide. Have a little sway from side to side, feeling how this loosens your hips and lower back. Next, turn the sway into a circle, moving your hips above your knees. Make the circle as big as feels comfortable. Practise this five times one way, and then five times the other way.

2. **Dog tail and cat.** Next, enjoy a stretch for the front and back of your body. Staying on all fours, breathe in, look forwards, draw your shoulders away from your ears. Imagine that you have a dog tail playfully stretching towards the sky, arch your back, moving your tummy towards the floor. Next, breathe out, bring your chin to your chest, round your back like an angry cat stretching and point your tail down low to the earth. Alternate between 'dog tail' and 'cat' five times, moving in time with your breath.

3. **Child's pose.** Now, sink your bottom towards your heels, stretch your arms out in front and place your forehead on the floor. Completely relax your legs. Stay in 'child's pose' for five to ten slow breaths, noticing the gentle stretch along your back. When you're ready, slowly return to all fours.

BE YOUR FUTURE FRIEND

We all have to do stuff we'd rather not do. It's just part of life. How can we make life's chores feel less of a bore? Let's use homework as our example.

If something, such as homework, has to be done, how you go about doing it makes all the difference. Refusing to do it is pointless and being resentful about it wastes time and energy. Try to find the good in the situation – the silver lining. How would doing this task now make life easier or better for your **FUTURE SELF**? When you have all the benefits of doing this task at the front of your mind, it will feel less boring!

Homework gives you a chance to develop skills and test yourself, which can make future exams easier and less stressful. Your **FUTURE SELF** is going to be grateful for the work you do **NOW** because you'll gain free time, confidence and new knowledge. Even if the task seems pointless, sitting down to do it builds stamina, determination and concentration. Throughout life you'll have to do things you don't enjoy now and again. You can resist them – or get them done and move onto things you enjoy more instead.

By getting into the right frame of mind, you will be better able to do the job carefully and effectively. Before you begin, make sure you aren't hungry or thirsty, so you can think straight. Sit up **TALL** so you feel poised and ready – slumping only makes you feel less like working. Do some chicken wing shoulder rolls (see page 23) if you're still feeling grouchy.

Make sure you're in a calm place: noise, chatter, screens and other people will only distract you.

Remaining focused only on the task at hand will make you far more productive. If you let yourself become distracted, jobs end up being left until the last minute, and this fritters away happiness, time and energy as they hang over your head. Get them done early and your Future Self won't feel so rushed or have to stay up late, and you'll enjoy having spare time to fill as you wish!

Pitch up with a positive attitude, get the job done with focus and drive, remembering how this helps your Future Self. Now you get to choose how you to reward yourself!

THE **WORLD** CAN **WAIT**

Sometimes, life can be so busy that we all need to chill and have a rest.

When our heads are spinning, a bit of rest can be all it takes to help us get back on track. If you feel tired and fed up, try the 'legs-up-the-wall' exercise (see page 181). First aiders put people in this position if they are in shock, because it makes all the blood flow to the heart and vital organs. It is just as useful for your mood and energy. Think of it as emotional first aid!

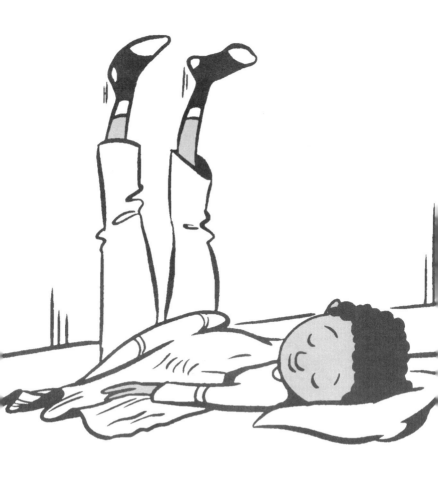

Grab a pillow and a blanket, take off your shoes and sit on the floor with your side facing the wall. Lie down onto your back and swing your legs up the wall so that both legs are fully supported by the wall and your bottom is as close to the wall as possible. Pop the pillow under your head and drape the blanket over your body for comfort. Now **RELAX**! Hang out here for five minutes, or longer if it feels good to you. Keep your mind focused on calm thoughts or your breath. Maybe listen to your calm playlist. Make sure there's proper relaxation in your week, and you'll keep your energy bank happily topped up.

GIVE **THANKS**

Feeling thankful gives us a lovely lift, but let's ramp that feeling up by sharing the warm and fuzzies with someone else! It can have an epic feel-good ripple effect.

3 STEPS **TO GIVING THE GIFT OF APPRECIATION**

1. **Give it some thought.** Think about someone who has shown you care and kindness. Enjoy thinking about all things they have done for you and how happy they make you feel. Now it's your turn to help them feel that way, too.

2. **Random acts of kindness.** Think about the little ways that you can communicate your thanks. It can be as simple as doing one of your sibling's chores for them, a kind word of encouragement, helping someone with their homework or inviting someone new to join your game. You could help out your parents by tidying up or doing the washing-up. How about getting creative by baking a cake to say thank you, gathering up a few flowers from the garden or painting a picture?

3. **Get writing!** Be super-specific and write a thank-you note. Remind your chosen person of the kind thing they did and what it meant to you. Deliver it in person or read it aloud to them to make it extra special. Recognise how it helps you both feel good and bonds you together in the process. Drink in all the positive vibes you've just created – this is the stuff that makes the world go round!

HUNT FOR TREASURE

There are so many things you can do to up your happiness, but the trick is to find what works best for you.

Now that you're nearly at the end of these pages, it's okay if not all of the tips, ideas and advice felt right for you. Just focus on what feels good for you at the moment. Our needs, interests and preferences are constantly changing, so don't be surprised if some different tips grabs you in the future. To bring all the bits that worked for you together, write down your own useful tips. It's time for one more list. This one is like a treasure map – the treasure being your **HAPPINESS**!

185

Flick through the book and identify the activities, hobbies, skills, yoga poses, ideas or sayings that have a positive impact on you. Map these out onto a big piece of paper using words or images. Hang it on your wall so that you see it every day.

Turn to your **TREASURE MAP** (see page 184) for things to do in your free time and to lift you up on tough days. Keep adding to it as you discover new techniques. Each time you dip into this book something might awaken your curiosity, so keep coming back to it like a wise friend.

Well done for making it to the end of the book! That's an achievement in itself. It's okay if it takes time to change your moods and habits. No one nails it instantly. While it can take some hard work, you're definitely worth the effort.

Notice, too, how small, positive acts can really make a **DIFFERENCE** to your day. There are loads of simple things you can do to help yourself feel confident and calm and to bring a big **SMILE** to your face. Take your time, and be kind to yourself as you practise these things. Remember, all of us are constantly learning.

As you move forwards, take a minute to look at how far you've come! Think about what you've learnt about yourself, reflect on things you've changed and all the ways that you have grown. Be proud of yourself. **You absolutely deserve to be happy.**

INDEX

ALSO AVAILABLE FROM WREN & ROOK

Paperback 978 1 5263 6153 0 | £6.99

E-book 978 1 5263 6152 3 | £6.99

ALSO AVAILABLE FROM WREN & ROOK